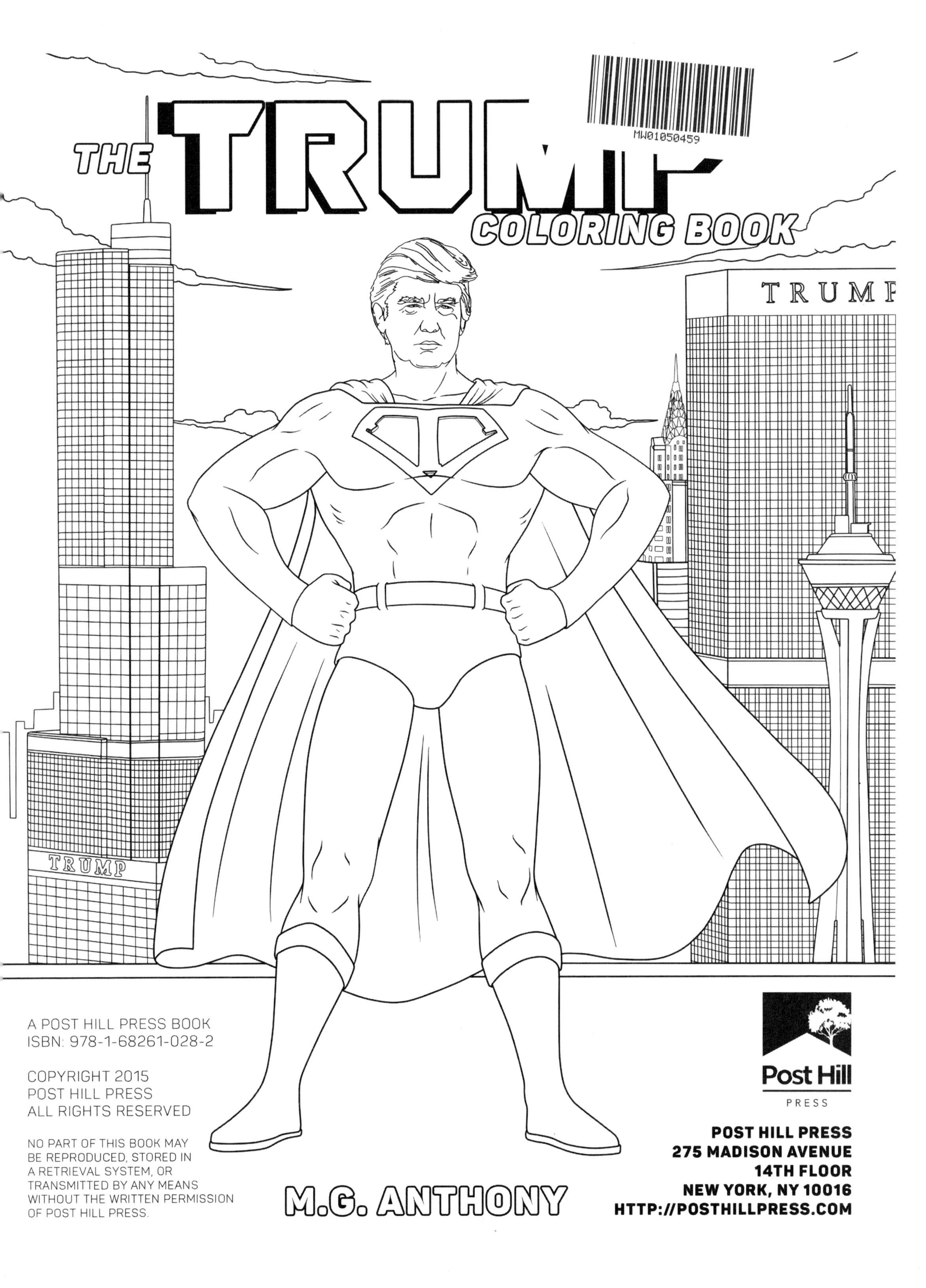

A POST HILL PRESS BOOK
ISBN: 978-1-68261-028-2

M.G. ANTHONY

Post Hill
PRESS

POST HILL PRESS
275 MADISON AVENUE
14TH FLOOR
NEW YORK, NY 10016
HTTP://POSTHILLPRESS.COM

UNITED

EXTRATERRESTRIAL
375
HIGHWAY

TRUMP

MAKE AMERICA
GREAT AGAIN
JULY
IV
MDCCLXXVI

REPUBLICAN
DEMOCRAT
CLINTON
TRUMP
SANDERS

YOU'RE FIRED!

THE WASHINGTON SQUARES

I WANT YOU
TO JOIN ME IN MAKING
AMERICA GREAT AGAIN

MAYFLOWER

E PLURIBUS UNUM

TUESDAY NIGHT
FEVER

We the People

$9\frac{3}{4}$
TRUMP EXPRESS
$9\frac{3}{4}$

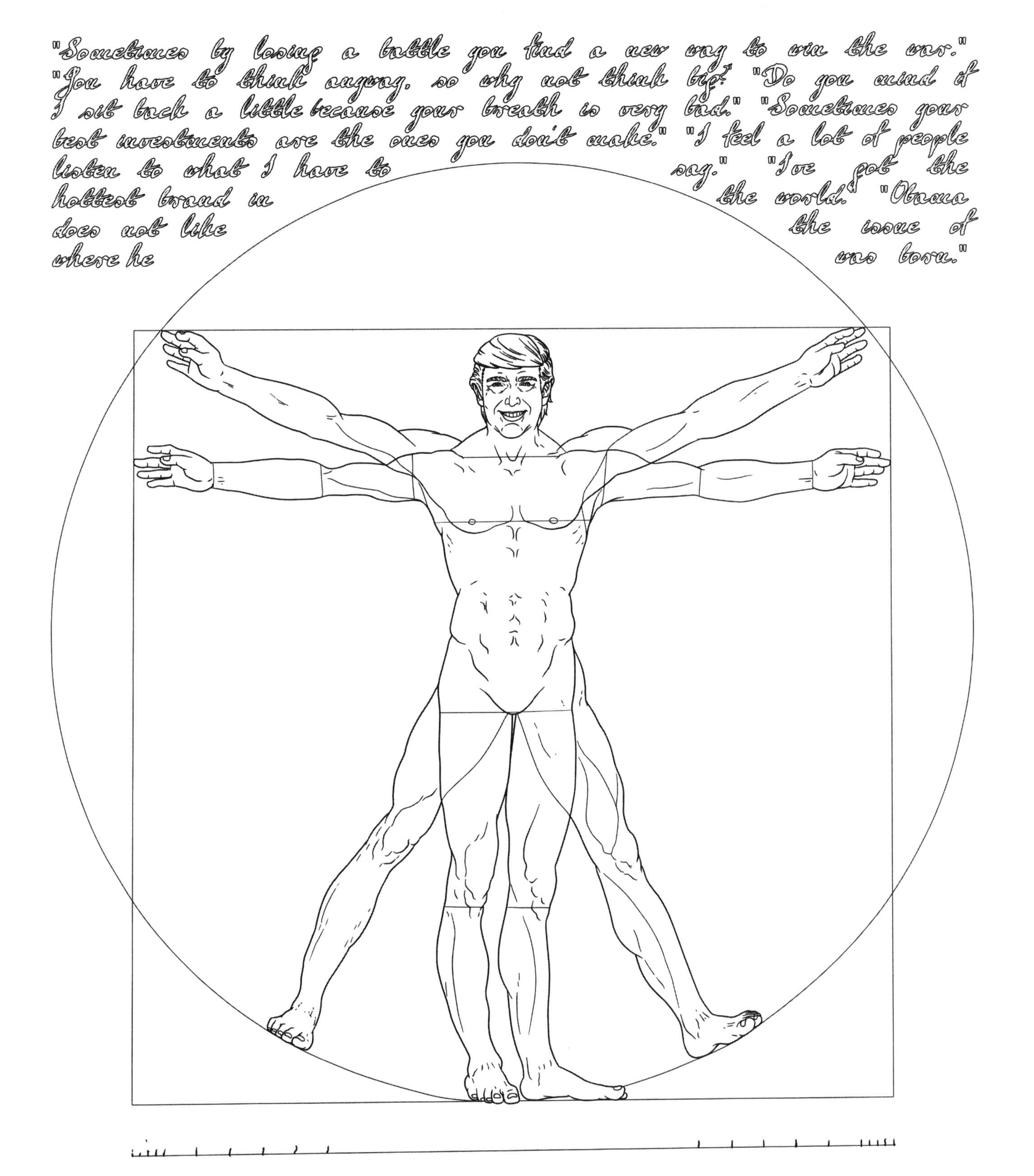

"I have a great relationship with the Mexican people." "I don't need anybody's money." "I have an attention span that's as long as it has to be." "Private jets cost a lot of money." "I built a great company, one of the - some of the most iconic assets in the world, $10 billion of net worth, more than $10 billion of net worth, and frankly, I had a great time doing it." "Our military has to be strengthened. Our vets have to be taken care of." "We have to end Obamacare, and we have to make our country great again, and I will do that."

past endpoint
of all
LIBHABER

SAL

DONALD TRUMP

LMW
281F

TRUMP
TRUMP
TRUMP
TRUMP
TRUMP
TRUMP
TRUMP
TRUMP
TRUMP

USS TRUMP

DT
20150100
A
ONE MILLION DOLLARS
FEDERAL RESERVE NOTE
1,000,000
T1
United States of America
T
USA
DONALD TRUMP
THE UNITED STATES OF AMERICA
TRUMP

TRUMP
GOLDEN TICKET
DATE
FEB.1
TIME
10 A.M.(SHARP)
PLACE
FRONT GATES

ENOLA
GAY

MISS
US

TRUMP FORCE ONE
86970

NO ENTRY

TRUMP

We Can Do It!

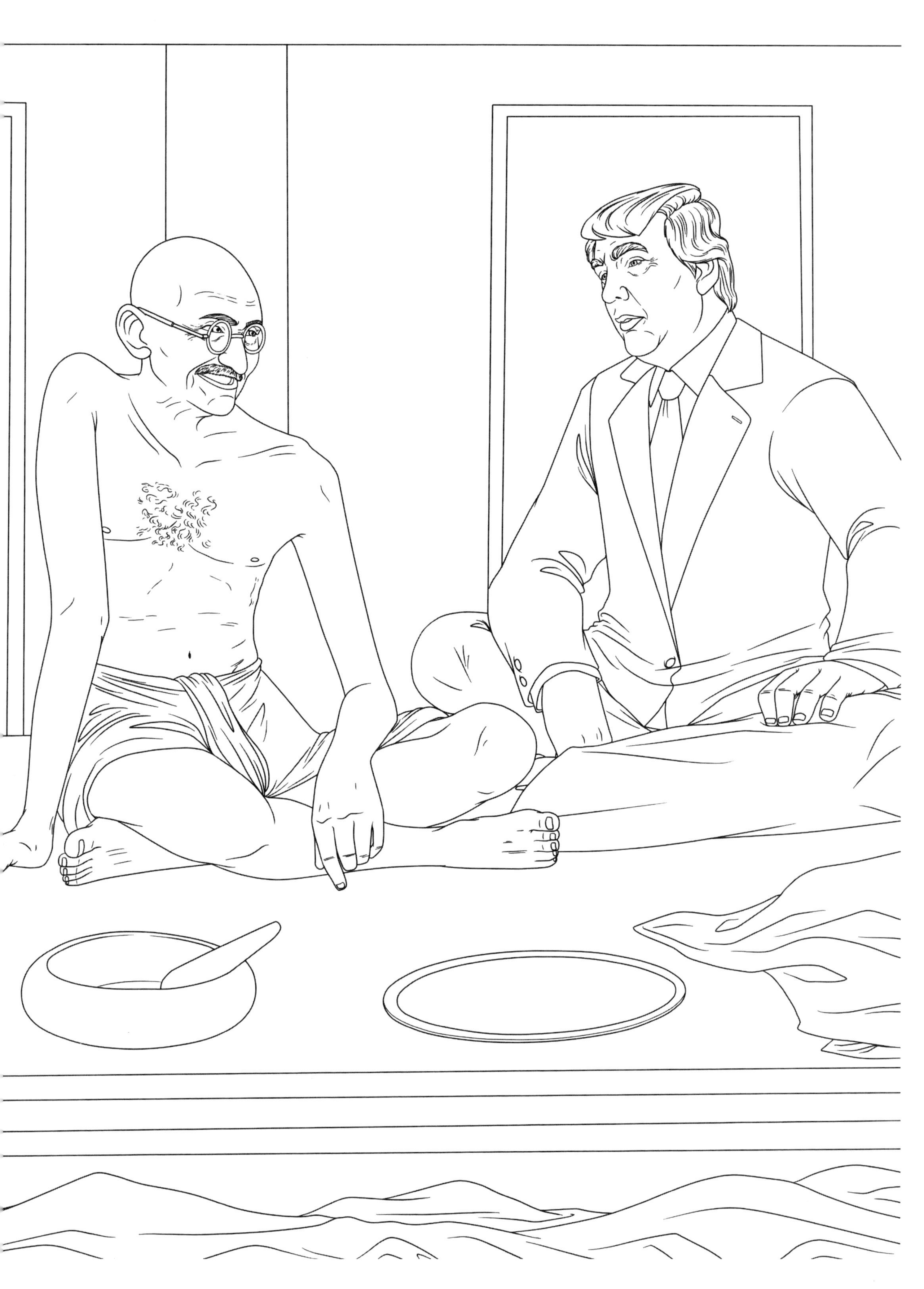

BOND